The American Civil War: 50 Fascinating Facts For Kids

Kevin Ashmole

All Rights Reserved. No part of this publication may be reproduced in any form or by any means, including scanning, photocopying, or otherwise without prior written permission of the copyright holder. Copyright Kevin Ashmole © 2014

This book is just one of a series of "Fascinating Facts For Kids" books. For more fascinating facts about people, history, animals, and much more please visit:

www.fascinatingfactsforkids.com

Contents

How the War Began............................ 1

Bull Run..4

General McClellan............................ 7

Confederate Invasion..........................9

Gettysburg.. 13

The War in the West........................... 16

The Siege of Vicksburg........................ 17

The Navy in the War............................19

The Siege of Petersburg....................... 20

March to the Sea & Surrender.............. 21

Lincoln's Death.................................. 24

Conclusion... 26

Illustration Attributions...................... 27

How the War Began

1. By the mid-19th century, almost 100 years after the United States was founded, many thousands of black Africans had been transported across the Atlantic Ocean and forced to work on the tobacco and cotton plantations of their new American masters.

Slaves working on a plantation

2. Although slaves were used in the northern United States, it was in the southern states that slavery was so important for the economy.

3. As time went on, the northern states brought in laws to abolish slavery, and the southern states became concerned that they would be forced to free their slaves. The issue of slavery was threatening to break up the Union and split the United States in two.

4. In 1860, Abraham Lincoln, a northern politician opposed to slavery, ran for the presidency of the United States. The southern states didn't trust Lincoln and threatened to leave the Union to form their own country if Lincoln was elected president.

Abraham Lincoln in 1860

5. Lincoln won the presidential election on November 6, 1860, with nearly all his votes coming from the northern states. Hardly anybody in the South had voted for him, and the southern states were to carry out their threat.

6. On December 20, South Carolina became the first state to leave the Union, and over the next few weeks six more states broke away from the North to form their own country, the "Confederate States of America."

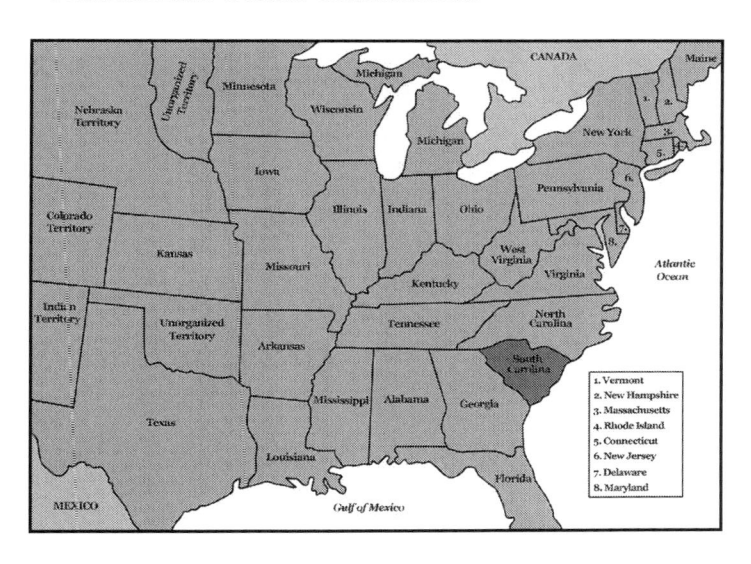

7. Lincoln was desperate to avoid a war between the northern states, which were known as the "Union," and the southern "Confederates," but on April 12, 1861, a Unionist fort was attacked in South Carolina. The American Civil War had begun.

Bull Run

8. Two days after the attack, Lincoln called for 75,000 volunteers to join the Union Army to stop the Confederate rebellion. This led to four more southern states leaving the Union, bringing the number of Confederate states to eleven.

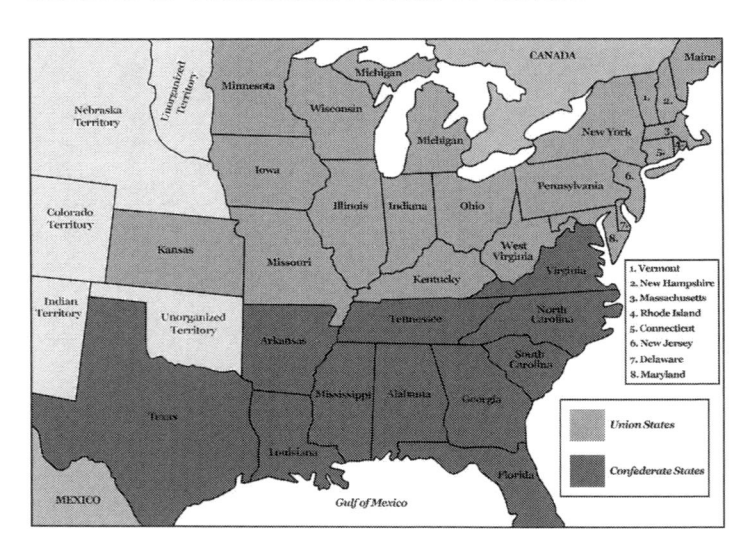

The northern and southern states

9. The Union was confident that it could defeat the South quickly and in July 1861, its Army, under the leadership of General Irvin McDowell, tried to capture the Confederate capital of Richmond, Virginia.

General McDowell

10. McDowell was a cautious man and had tried to convince Lincoln that his men, who were not professional soldiers, were not yet ready for battle. But Lincoln knew that the Confederates were in the same position and ordered McDowell to march towards Richmond.

11. The Confederate Army was ready and waiting, and the two Armies met in the first major battle of the war on July 21, at the "First Battle of Bull Run" (also known as the "First Battle of Manassas") just twenty-five miles (40 km) from the Unionist capital of Washington.

The "First Battle of Bull Run"

12. The Confederate Army defeated the Unionists, forcing them to retreat back to Washington, in what was the worst battle ever fought on American soil up until then. More than 800 men were killed and more than 2,500 injured. The Union now realized that it had a fight on its hands and that the war would not be a short one.

General McClellan

13. Following the First Battle of Bull Run, Lincoln removed General McDowell from his command and replaced him with General George McClellan, ordering him to turn his soldiers into a disciplined and organized Army.

14. General McClellan built his "Army of the Potomac" into a well drilled force which was used to defend Washington as well as fighting the Confederates. Lincoln rewarded McClellan by promoting him to "General-in-Chief" of the whole Union Army in November 1861.

General McClellan

15. McClellan proved too cautious for Lincoln, and when he finally made an attempt to capture Richmond, his Army was defeated in a series of battles lasting the seven days from June 25 to July 1, 1862.

16. The important victory by the Confederates in the "Seven Days Battle" ensured that the war would continue for some time. Lincoln had been looking for a general to end the war quickly, and he removed McClellan from the post of "General-in-Chief," replacing him with Major-General Henry Halleck.

Confederate Invasion

17. The two Armies met again on August 28 at the "Second Battle of Bull Run", and after three days of fierce fighting the Union Army suffered another defeat. Over 20,000 men were killed or injured, with nearly twice as many casualties on the Union side.

The "Second Battle of Bull Run"

18. Robert E. Lee, the commander of the Confederate Army in Virginia, now saw an opportunity to invade the North, and he began the march towards Washington.

Robert E. Lee

19.   General McClellan and his "Army of the Potomac" stopped Lee's progress near the town of Sharpsburg, Maryland, where another bloody battle took place on September 17. The "Battle of Sharpsburg," also called the "Battle of Antietam," resulted in a much-needed victory for the Union at the cost of more than 22,000 dead or wounded on both sides.

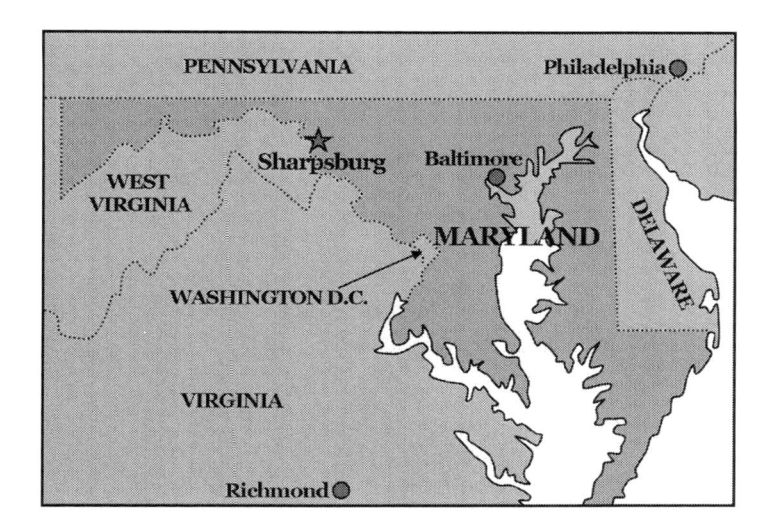

20. Lee and his Army retreated back to the South, and McClellan's failure to follow them resulted in Lincoln replacing him again with a new general, Ambrose E. Burnside.

21. Another devastating defeat for the Union Army came in December at the "Battle of Fredericksburg," after which both Armies paused the fighting for the rest of the winter. It seemed that the Union generals were good at organizing and planning, but lacked nerve on the battlefield.

The "Battle of Fredericksburg"

Gettysburg

22. The following May, the Union Army suffered yet another defeat to the Confederates at the "Battle of Chancellorsville," after which General Lee invaded the North for a second time.

23. The next meeting of the two opposing Armies was at Gettysburg, Pennsylvania, and the battle that took place was to become the most famous of the war. Nearly 8,000 men were killed and more than 27,000 wounded over three days from July 1-3, 1863.

The "Battle of Gettysburg"

24. Gettysburg turned out to be a decisive victory for the Union, and Lee was forced to retreat back to the South. The Confederate Army would not invade the North again.

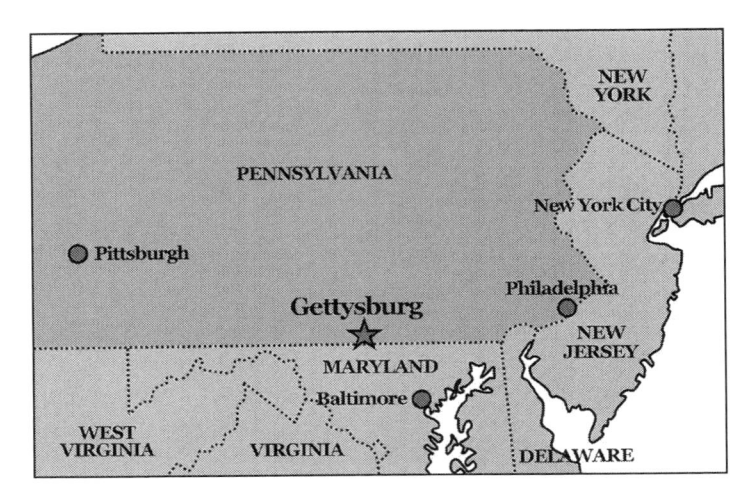

25. Four and a half months after the battle, on November 19, Lincoln traveled to Gettysburg to honor the men who had died, and he gave a speech to a crowd of 20,000 people. The speech, known as the "Gettysburg Address," lasted less than three minutes, during which time Lincoln gave his reasons why the war was so important for the freedom and equality of everyone in America. The speech (below) has become one of the most important in the history of the United States:

<u>The Gettysburg Address – November 19, 1863</u>

"Four score and seven years ago our fathers brought forth on this continent a new nation,

conceived in liberty, and dedicated to the proposition that all men are created equal. Now we are engaged in a great civil war, testing whether that nation, or any nation so conceived and so dedicated, can long endure. We are met on a great battlefield of that war. We have come to dedicate a portion of that field, as a final resting place for those who here gave their lives that that nation might live. It is altogether fitting and proper that we should do this.

But, in a larger sense, we can not dedicate, we can not consecrate, we can not hallow this ground. The brave men, living and dead, who struggled here, have consecrated it, far above our poor power to add or detract. The world will little note, nor long remember what we say here, but it can never forget what they did here. It is for us the living, rather, to be dedicated here to the unfinished work which they who fought here have thus far so nobly advanced. It is rather for us to be here dedicated to the great task remaining before us - that from these honored dead we take increased devotion to that cause for which they gave the last full measure of devotion - that we here highly resolve that these dead shall not have died in vain - that this nation, under God, shall have a new birth of freedom - and that government of the people, by the people, for the people, shall not perish from the earth."

The War in the West

26. The attempts to capture Washington and Richmond took place in the eastern part of the country, but the Armies in the West also played an important part in the war.

27. The Mississippi River, which flows over 2,000 miles (3,200 km) from the north of the United States to the Gulf of Mexico in the South, was important to the southern states for transporting food and livestock.

28. The Union had captured the southern port of New Orleans in May 1862, and if they could take control of the whole river, they would cut the South in two.

The Siege of Vicksburg

29. The Confederates had a fortress at the city of Vicksburg, which overlooked the Mississippi from a height of 200 feet (60 meters). Its 200 guns could fire on any Union boat that was passing by. It was vital for the Union Army to capture Vicksburg.

30. The Union Army, led by Major-General Ulysses S. Grant, attacked Vicksburg on two occasions but was driven back both times. The city's height above the river made it virtually impossible to capture, so Grant decided to surround the city to prevent food and other supplies reaching it.

The "Siege of Vicksburg"

31. The "Siege of Vicksburg" lasted forty-eight days from May 18 until July 4, when the Confederates surrendered. This victory, along with the Union victory at Gettysburg, was a turning point of the war.

The Navy in the War

32. Along with the Armies, the Navies also played an important part in the war, particularly the Union Navy, which was much larger than that of the Confederates. Lincoln's General-in-Chief in the early stages of the war, Winfield Scott, came up with a plan to use the Navy to help defeat the South.

33. Scott's plan, known as the "Anaconda Plan," was to have Union ships blockade the Confederate seaports and surround its coast, to stop important supplies getting through to the southern states. Towns and cities along the length of the Mississippi would also be captured to leave the Union in control of this important waterway.

34. Scott retired from the Army early on in the war and the plan was modified, but in April 1862, a fleet of Union ships captured the port of New Orleans at the mouth of the Mississippi.

35. Following the capture of New Orleans, the fleet sailed up the Mississippi capturing other towns on the way. Meanwhile, another fleet of Union ships was sailing down the river from the north. When Vicksburg was finally taken after the forty-eight-day siege in July 1863, the Mississippi was under the control of the Union, and the South was split in two.

The Siege of Petersburg

36. Following a victory for the Union at Chattanooga in November 1863, Lincoln made General Grant his commander of the whole Union Army, and he began to plot a campaign that would bring the final defeat of the Confederates. It seemed that Lincoln had at last found a general he could trust.

37. Grant planned to capture Richmond and fought further bloody battles against General Lee's Confederates, who retreated to the town of Petersburg, twenty miles (30 km) south of Richmond. As he had done at Vicksburg, General Grant put Petersburg under a siege, this one lasting for nine months.

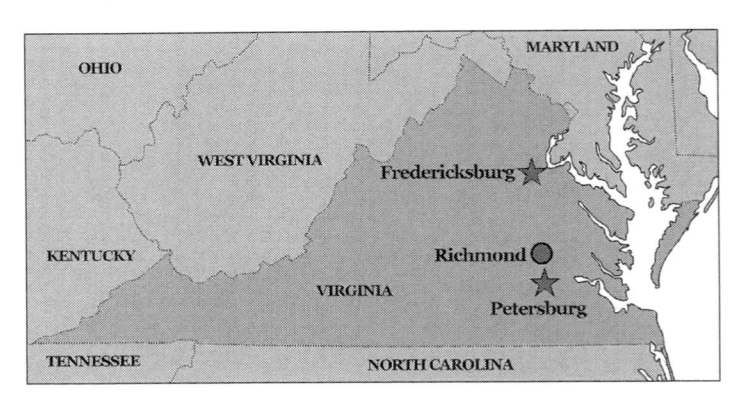

March to the Sea & Surrender

38. With much of the Confederate Army under siege in Petersburg, Grant was able to send one of his Union Armies deep into enemy territory to the south.

39. Led by Major-General William T. Sherman, the Union Army invaded Georgia from the northwest before capturing the city of Atlanta on September 1, 1864.

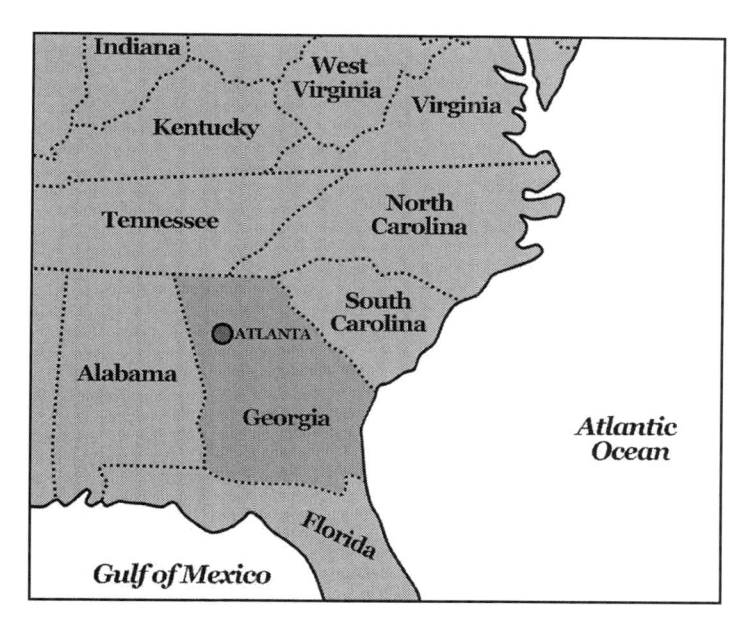

40. In November, General Sherman and his soldiers began what has since become known as the "March to the Sea." Before leaving Atlanta, Sherman ordered the population to leave, and he then had the city burned to the ground.

41. By marching from Atlanta to the Atlantic coast Sherman planned to divide the Confederacy in two, and by destroying as much as they could on the way, the morale of both the Army and the civilian population would be broken. On reaching the coast he could then head north to help out General Grant's Army in Petersburg.

42. Sherman's Army spread itself out for sixty miles (100 km) and marched the 285 miles (460 km) to the coast, marching into the city of Savannah at dawn on December 21.

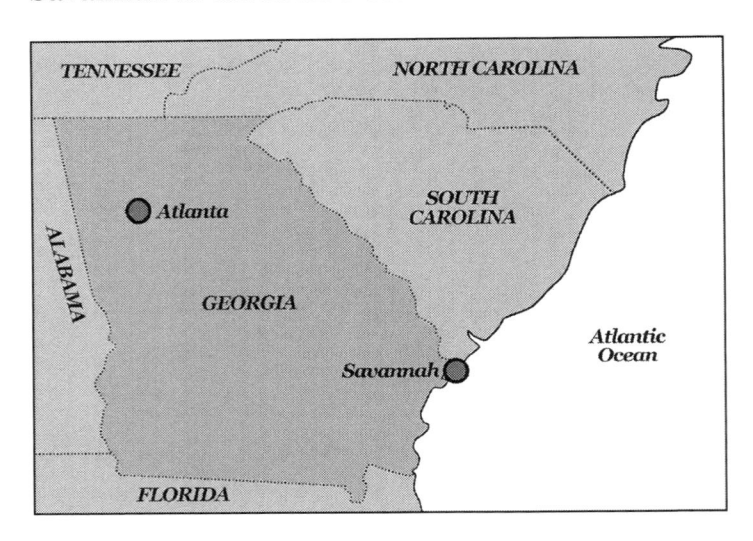

43. Back at Petersburg, Grant's siege tactics were working. With no supplies getting through, the Confederates eventually evacuated both Petersburg and Richmond on April 2, 1865, retreating westwards along the Appomattox

River, pursued by Grant and his Army. Seven days later, on April 9, Lee surrendered to Grant.

44. Following the taking of Savannah, Sherman and his men headed north, pushing back Confederate forces on their way. The Confederate commander, General Joseph Johnston eventually surrendered on April 26, 1865, and after four long years, the bloodiest war in American history was over.

Lincoln's Death

45. On April 14, 1865, President Lincoln and his wife visited Ford's Theater in Washington to see a play called "Our American Cousin." They arrived late at about 8.30 in the evening, and although the play had already started, the audience stood up to cheer the president, who then sat down to enjoy the performance.

46. Around ninety minutes later, John Wilkes Booth, a Confederate who hated Lincoln, entered the president's box and crept up behind him. He pulled out a gun, aimed it at the president's head and pulled the trigger.

Lincoln's Assassination

47. As Lincoln slumped forward, Booth jumped out of the box onto the stage below and although he broke a leg as he did so, he still managed to escape. He was on the run for twelve days before being caught and killed in a struggle.

48. The president was taken from the theater to a house across the street where doctors tried to save him. But there was nothing they could do and Lincoln died at 7.22 the next morning.

49. Lincoln was the first United States president to have been assassinated and America was in shock. Thousands of people came to Washington from all over the country to pay their respects.

50. Lincoln's body was taken to his family home in Illinois by train. Hundreds of thousands of people lined the track and attended memorial services on the journey. He was buried in Springfield on May 3, 1865.

Lincoln's tomb in Springfield

Conclusion

The Civil War was the bloodiest war in American history, claiming the lives of 600,000 men and causing countless casualties.

After the war there was a strong desire for forgiveness, so that the country could be rebuilt and the unity that had once existed be restored. Not everyone shared this dream though - many in the North thought that the South should be severely punished.

A lasting legacy of the war was the abolishment of slavery - the government had passed the 13th amendment in April 1865, making slavery illegal.

America had come through the worst time in its history and was ready for any challenge ahead. Over the next 150 years she was to emerge as the most powerful country on Earth, and a defender of democracy and freedom for all.

Illustration Attributions

Slaves working on a plantation
New York Historical Society [Public domain]

General McDowell
{{PD-US}}

The "First Battle of Bull Run"
Kurz & Allison [Public domain]
{{PD-US}}

General McClellan
Mathew Brady [Public domain]

General Halleck
{{PD-US}}

The "Second Battle of Bull Run"
{{PD-US}}

General Lee
{{PD-US}}

The "Battle of Fredericksburg"
www.goodfreephotos.com

The "Battle of Gettysburg"
Adam Cuerden
{{PD-US}}

The "Siege of Vicksburg"
Kurz & Allison [Public domain]
{{PD-US}}

Lincoln's Assassination
Currier and Ives [Public domain]
Kurz & Allison [Public domain]
{{PD-US}}

Made in the USA
Columbia, SC
24 November 2023